R Wars of the Roses

OTHER POETRY BY DAVID TIPTON

Poems in Transit (1960)
City of Kings (1967)
Millstone Grit (1972)
Pachacamac (1974)
Black Clough (1975)
Departure in Yellow (1976)
Graph of Love (1976)
Nomads and Settlers (1980)
Facts and Fantasies (1980)
Moving House (1982)
Doors — *with 6 other poets* — (1982)
Roc y Mimosa (1983)

WARS OF THE ROSES

DAVID TIPTON

 RIVELIN GRAPHEME PRESS
BRADFORD & LONDON 1984

ACKNOWLEDGEMENTS

Some of these poems first appeared in the following magazines:
Affinities, Diversion, Global Tapestry, Hard Lines, Palantir, Pennine Platform, Poetry Nottingham, Manx Graffiti and *Sheaf.*

For Tish

SECTION 1

SPRING 1979

1

The museum of the Green Howards, their memorial tower built
        into Trinity Church,
the Grey Friars monastery dissolved by Thomas Cromwell,
a cold wind, the children thirsty, Patrick white as a sheet
        from the twisting road through the dales.
Walked round the castle walls above the arched bridge
the Swale between trees   white and turbulent over rocks,
Robin Hood's Tower built by Rufus, the Norman earl:
I remembered it well, a solace even then in sombre winter.

Drove north along the A1, through the Tyne tunnel to Berwick
the North Sea actually blue as we strolled over dunes
        and hard sand
scaled the wall, the cat on a lead sniffing the sea's tang.
Alongside the coast   Firth (fiord estuary) of Forth
        Lindisfarne
St Aidan and the Benedictines a 'lamp of Christianity'
        despite the Danes,
through border country in the early evening
battleground of English and Scottish kings.

2

After seven years Martin's cottage had changed, the big barn
        a living-room
with parquet floor   persian rugs   a wood fire
drinking wine   dining on humus and beef casserole
getting drunk and adjusting to the changes created by the
        years
his text-books bestsellers in the Islamic world.
Twenty years before a young poet crossing the Andes by bus,
        shipping to Peru, redbearded and beat,
sitting in the bows of a paddle-steamer up the Paraná,
        exploring Asunción
the smell of burning *quebracho*, rosewood and eucalyptus.
We've talked so often over wine   poetry and relationships
both born under the same sign   earthy, sensual and pleasure-
        seeking but....

Down the bank to the Tyne, the East Linton bridge and the
        church
reddish sandstone   dried crimson-lake
the river tumbling with power and ferocity through the narrow
        gorge
tons of white water with the odour of peat
pell-mell over cascades   carrying all before it
whirlpool and eddy   into the sluggish pool
before meandering to the sea
'I've seen salmon leaping up this ravine,' it's almost
        unbelievable
nothing could survive those twenty yards it seemed.

In the sandstone pub we plan new projects and a press
the four children sleeping in the cottage
the past is always present   there's no escaping it
        or need to
the poem can contain it all and control it if organic
and unrestrained by literary inhibition.

3

Edinburgh and cold rain on the hill above Holyrood
spoils our picnic. We drive into the city
at a delicatessen aromatic with Earl Grey tea, cheese
        and ground coffee
the Italian owner in a Scottish accent offers us a taste
        of the fish we plan to buy,
I cannot always separate images from memories of previous
        visits
once with an Irish girl   her heavy chestnut hair and wide
        hips
whom I treated shabbily at the urging of another woman
Martin remembers her with warmth   I think that if things
        had been different
we might have...but the end could have been worse as it
        so often is
'the confusions of a melancholy poet'
we went round the castle, from its high walls the city
        spreading out towards the Firth
the big gun from the Great War, the children's questions,
soldiers stood around in tartan trousers, dirk and claymore,
draught beer from a bodega, the Gothic turrets and high
        gables
'but the influence was French...'

Knox and the Calvinists, Mary Queen of Scots in bed with
       her lover, Bothwell,
and across the city Hearts were losing to Hibernian
while from the ramparts, floodlit in summer, a cold wind
       through the battlements
'*Peru beat Scotland 3-1 in Argentina,*' Tish said,
Siobhan seven years ago   the white skin of redheads,
that old blue-movie of the senses back to the sandstone
       village.

Everything passes and fear of death pierces unexpectedly
       like an arrow from a crossbow,
bones buried beneath battlefields, the earth scouring
       what the scavengers leave
yet human history if you take as David Attenborough did
       a year as your scale of 'life on earth'
is a mere few minutes, so we get drunk again and plan to
       get it down,
begin in 1908 or some such arbitrary date, social history
       and family anecdote,
weave the personal into your chronicle, a geography of the
       mind and a science of emotion
as we stroll along the beach with our bags and hamper
       I see it complete
a stained-glass window or an illuminated manuscript
the book to hand down, passing on your genes
       an algebraic equation.
It is his poem or mine, journal or myth.

4

Out to Seacliffe Bay where Martin points out Bass Rock. We
       guess its distance from the shore
and under-estimate. St Baldred's Cave, I forget the legend
       though we were told it.

After the picnic Kate feeds the baby — it must be cold
    though we're sheltered by the bluff,
an arm of cliff and the smell of rocks at low tide,
seaweed, samphire and innumerable little pools that we
    explore,
Martin ahead jumping from rock to rock.

The sea's cold yet gentle, reddish sea-anemones cling to
    red sandstone,
I skim pebbles across the water, a series of small splashes
    which the kids count,
starfish, tiny crabs and sea-spiders in pairs,
jelly-like blobs of roe or spawn in pools *'it's funny stuff'*
water tastes salty with a hint of ice. I've written so much
    about the beach
but it's over a year since I've explored sea-wrack and rock
    pool.

Martin has just returned from Mexico, two months ago he was
    on a boat up the Nile,
travel's easier these days, the world's a smaller place,
egalitarianism has disadvantages, but so has elitism,
*'you veer between cliché and contradiction, you have opinions
    but no ideas.'*
I've not been abroad except for one week in Venice for ten
    years,
place is an act of imagination, you have become a mental
    traveller seeking roots.
We stroll to the far headland and clamber over rocks
unexpectedly come upon the Gegan — a small harbour built
    by smugglers,
a sharp turn from the narrow inlet between black rock
    invisible from the bay,
the coastguard cutter, kegs of brandy from France, whiskey
    to Berwick.

Back along the sand the bones of a rabbit, dead gulls and
    gannets
tarred by oil dumped in the estuary by tankers
and further along the government's erecting another nuclear-
    power plant
there'll be demonstrations and protest.

The bay is untouched and lovely from the car,
there are six novels and various long poems that you must
        complete,
always this compulsion, the blank page to be filled,
I keep telling you it's the plurality of things and you have
        to keep the record straight
record facts and phenomena, a palimpsest which suggests
        form and style
even within the apparently formless.

5

Most of the day it rains. Martin works in his study, I read,
        the cat sniffs rats in the field,
the kids make jigsaws, Annabel — a chubby toddler — follows
        my eleven-year old son around the cottage.
We clamber down to the river's edge and try to dislodge two
        barrels trapped against a log
trapped across the gorge. Cold water rushes by. Every so often
a blue and cream train hurtles towards Edinburgh or south
        and frightens the cats.
I compare the sandstone of the bridge with the reddish wall
        of a tall house,
the church bells chime. We take some snaps down by the river
and Martin cooks a curry which we eat until we're more than
        full,
drink beer   wine   tequila   sit by the fire looking at a
        book
full of photographs of Nubian desert-tribes — black bodies
        gleam with sweat,
steatopygous buttocks and the breasts of young girls.
The kids watch TV and Tish takes Thai Two for a midnight
        breath of air,
we play chess and Martin with unexpected caution and patience
        beats me.
It's gone midnight. The fire's died and the beer bottles
        are all empty,
ashtrays full of butts, the children asleep. We go to bed,
we're all on our own, of course, but together and protected
        by an easy-going warmth.

6

Kate waves us off outside the sandstone cottage,
we drive north-west across the Forth Bridge, get lost on
    minor roads to Stirling,
the castle on the hill, snow in patches on the heights
through Dunblane and Braco, the stone farmhouse — Silverton
    isolated.
Thinner-haired, still-bearded, Alan, a friend I've known
    for forty years
and who's shared much with me one way or another
though we've not seen each other for ages   greets me.
We talk of old acquaintances, eat sandwiches and scones
    with Australian lager.
If I write that poem Alan will figure in it, I remember
primary school in wartime Birmingham, fights on the Common,
    cricket on the hilltop,
early girlfriends and teaching in a comprehensive school
    together.
We walk down the lane, over the bridge that crosses Allan
    Water
between the Ochil Hills and Trossack Glens
to the Roman fort, outpost of the IX Legion,
elaborately trenched and fortified to north and east.
The kids find a hare's skull, there are six lines of outer
    stockade,
frontier country, Caledonians in the highlands, bronze
    against steel,
these islands a rich vein as yet scarcely mined or tapped.
Unbelievably this is the furthest north I've been, in the
    past always that pull towards the tropics.
A rabbit runs up the slope, vanishes in bracken. There were
    rats in the farm
until they acquired their black cat. Tish takes Thai Two
    with us on the walk,
he sniffs the tantalising odours on the breeze.

We have to leave, driving through the lowlands in squalls
    of rain,
the names of Scottish football clubs,
through the Tweedsmuir pass, the high fells and Green Lowther
along the Eden valley — more snow here than further north,
bleak but bronzed in lingering twilight
south-east via Settle and the dales to Bradford.

7

Maureen arrives from Arizona, my divorce and hers, friends
    and projects
difficulties of translation, the arrogance of certain poets.
She buys black lentils, split peas, coriander, cumin,
we drive around the city, the birthplace of the Brontës,
    the 3 and 5-rise locks
and the model village of Saltaire with its almshouse and
    mill in yellow stone,
Sir Titus Salt the textile magnate, friend of philanthropists
    and reformers,
created a link with Peru importing alpaca and llama,
soft water flowing from the dales for washing and dyeing
    the wool.
The narrow cobbled street to the vicarage at Haworth,
a fierce wind off the moors, hail, sleet and snow
'no wonder they all died of pneumonia, weak lungs or alcohol,'
talking about the rages of Rochester's wife,
a sensual woman inspired by sexual energy, or the single
    spirochete in the bloodstream.
Sitting in the kitchen, green trousers and red Indian waist-
    coat,
waiting for the others to arrive, we talk of the macabre,
Peruvian food simmering on the stove.

8

After checking through our old translations we drove up
    to Ilkley,
climbed up by the beck to the cascade and triangular
    copse,
Tish hobbling on her damaged ankle which gave way in her
    high-heeled brown boots,
making love earlier that afternoon between writing these
    journals,
white sturdy thighs, pert bottom, black smudge of hair.
Up to Bolton Abbey, the stepping-stones covered, black
    and white sheep on the slope,
Augustinian and self-sufficient, dissolved by Cromwell,
    razed save for the church
and once-visited by Wordsworth, the view to Barden Bridge
    beautiful
the meeting of the waters and on up the winding road,
valley of desolation, high moors in rust, cinnamon and
    sepia
to Grassington's narrow grey streets in weak sunlight,
the high plateau, reservoirs, Blubberhouses and down.

9

Hadrian and Constantine, the Danes and Normans, 1328 Edward
    married Philippa here,
the Jews were massacred in the 12th century and York surrendered
    to Cromwell after Marston Moor,
1644 Stafford executed, Robinson Crusoe 'born' here and *Tristram
    Shandy* published by John Hinxman sign of the Bible
    in Stonegate,
stained-glass transept and nave, chapter house and choir, five
    pale jade translucent sisters,
the arches of the crypt, lancet window, stone shields of barons
    who met in 1310,
statues of kings and the Black Prince.

Shivering we wandered round, snow in the north wind blowing
    through the city,
lunched outside the pub flooded last winter by the Ouse,
Samuel Smith bitter, then along the twisting Shambles,
Richard of York's head on a lance at Micklegate,
to the Castle Museum, its debtors' prison where I'd have lain,
    black jet
and the cobbled 18th century street — the London to York stage
    held up by Dick Turpin
and a parking fine around Edward's white walls, saffron
    daffodils on the grass below,
an icy wind on the road to Ripon and above Pately Bridge
the moors and high fells under crisp snow in early May,
    slush on the roads home.

10

Snow on the moors through the study window out to Baildon
    and Windhill
where all morning we translated, rested a day
and drove up to Fountains Abbey more beautiful than I
    remembered it,

Benedictine then Cistercian, elaborate design and layout,
the Skell running through its south side, vaulted refactory
        and calefactory,
with a good sewage system and central-heating for the Abbot's
        house
the monks' dorter and frater,
where Robin Hood disputed right of way with an itinerant
        friar,
a sanctuary of gracious living, '*a 12th century Hilton*' as
        Cressie said.
If lucky we would have been monks or literate lay-brothers
or perhaps fought under the Black Prince at Poitiers and
        Crecy,
or outlaws in Lincoln-green mantle, deer-skin boots, tunic
        and feathered cap,
sword and longbow, poaching the King's forests,
fishing the beck, resting in the infirmary or the Abbot's
        prison,
insanitary water and rotten food, black death and the pox.

Serfs drifted to the towns or sought those peripatetic bands
        in the wilds
which we drove through once again to the castle battlements
        above the Swale
for sandwiches and yoghurt sheltered from the wind that
        nipped through blue denim.
Among greenery the ruins of Jervaulx Abbey, rain and sleet,
Middleham Castle a brief halt, Warwick the Kingmaker and
        Richard of York,
the White Rose ascendant, crossing the Ure
and along the Swale, rugged mountains and desolate moors
        under snow,
a spectacular view of high fells out of Muker,
        Lovely Seat and Great Shunner,
into Hawes and heavy snow to Windermere, the A65 home in
        gathering light,
fish and chips, beer, warm rooms and books on the Middle
        Ages.

SECTION 2

SUMMER 1979

11

All the long June day watching television
the trooping of the Colours for the Queen's birthday
red black and gold, drum bagpipe and bugle, the symmetry
    and pattern
then Mike Hendrick bowling out the Pakistan XI and an Asif
    Iqbal fifty
while cats roll in the dust and hunt birds in the snicket,
after rain a song thrush on the roof where all day
people have been voting in the EEC elections.
No nostalgia for that time when half the world was red
    on the map,
the railways in India and Argentina, a kind of justice
    to the far-flung corners
and a legacy that included cricket.
I'm not becoming either more patriotic or conservative
but am bored with the arguments and obsessions
that for so long have possessed me   recall two years with
    the Colours in Malaya
the easy financial transaction in houses out-of-bounds,
the bitter-sweet joy at a simple level, sharing with no-one,
    a solitary experience
senses sharp, the fragrance of spice or sperm
that green-and-purple ribbon on khaki, a tattoo of crossed
    kukris
up-country between kampong and river with fifty rounds
    of ammo round the waist.

12

One night in June, drunk, walking the dark streets home
a rash of orange lights in the valley
the black-green and mottled shadows of the park
arguing about the same old things   *'women are never free'*
> you say,
'alone I couldn't do this for fear of rape or worse,
men are moslems at heart or boasters ennumerating their
> *achievements,*
that century of cunts in which they've stuck their silly
> *cocks...'*
It is a warm June night, a rash of orange lights in the
> valley,
listening I try to interpret and decide to write
poems of landscape or physical activity...
'I'm just being studied for your next novel
a specimen pinned to your literary ambition
to be dissected, analysed and tabulated...'

The sun set over the moors while I was sitting at the desk
dreaming not of women, but of sea travel, distant ports,
those parts of the world I've never seen.
The poems that still please me are descriptive and detached,
clean like the curve of a leaping dolphin
or the blue disk of sea from a ship in mid-Atlantic.

13

The emotions sometimes lie (the romantic lie)
all right I've written some jejune and sentimental poems
though they seemed true enough at the time
reacting to dissolving tenderness or tenderness offered
> once again,

better to be objective — the body changes
and it takes more exercise to burn off the beer
        and carbohydrates
but attitudes remain approximately the same
that vision of the loveless solitary, skin like old leather,
on the waterfront at Macao or some such seedy port —
another species of lie. What do you really want?
Not to be baffled by the demanding appetites
nor blinded by that conjuring trick of the senses.
The stance should be mocking and sardonic
like Byron's or some such romantic satirist.

14

It's raining, the monsoons have come, Market Street a river
        in flood,
in the yellow Renault I meet Jim Burns by the Alhambra,
        he's slimmer than I remember,
back home we talk of Kerouac and the Beats,
Allan Burgis shows us his photographs of poets,
overlooking the stream at Burbage and towards Higger Tor
        I look slimmer then
thinned by adrenalin, metabolism quickened by disintegrating
        marriage.
It's four years ago. My son, Jonathan, had just been born
and I was on the verge of making several bad decisions.
After beer and curry we drive to Ilkley in the rain
watch Francis score the winning goal for Forest in the
        European Cup
then read our poems to a tiny gathering in the *Candy Room*.
I scarcely remember driving home, but in the morning
talking of who said what to whom and where and when
they tell me I stopped and swerved to avoid a badger in the
        road.

15

'*Love is illusion*' — did I say that? I don't know, this
    collage has quotes from various sources,
'*you've put on weight,*' he said while playing croquet,
'*a sure sign you're not in love for that burns up the fat,*'
'*I could fuck anyone from sixteen to sixty,*'
but then we all have the instincts of gigolo or whore,
    anonymity with strangers
only later when subtleties set in and fantasies evaporate
does the simple act become embroidered like a frieze,
the Bayeux tapestry with its archers and knights,
difficult to unravel or disentangle from the documentary
    evidence
the petitions and pleas that crop up in divorce courts
or on the psychoanalyst's couch if you have resources.

16

We drive in the yellow Renault to Todmorden
meet Jeff and Tony in the pub to discuss *Grape Notes*,
    Apple Music,
afterwards on the hills high up above this weird town
    of mills and stone
straggling along the Calder valley, a monument to the
    Industrial Revolution,
we make out in the hot afternoon, bare buttocks in the sun,
walk across fields, over the beck, scale fences into the
    well-kept mansion,
drive home but return to search for your bracelet with the
    blue stone and silver rings
and by accident take a B-road up through Heptonstall
emerge suddenly in a wild moorland with streams and cloughs
    waterfall and cascade   peat and small lakes
only a few miles from the lights of Colne and Nelson on the
    Pennine border,
the Wars of the Roses, and down for a drink in a town on the
    Aire,

home to find your jewelry exactly where you'd left it
  on a shelf near the kitchen sink
and over Chinese food from the take-away I pore over an
  Ordnance Survey map
to locate our route in the yellow Renault.

17

With wristwork and elegance Zaheer and Majid dominate the
  West Indian attack,
Richards scores a century, England lose 4-2 to Austria,
  Borg is almost beaten by Amritraj,
Jeremy Thorpe's acquitted and various atrocities fill the
  papers.
Britain's love affair with the Indian subcontinent absorbs
  us
— the Khyber Pass and E.M. Forster, religions along the
  Ganges and poverty in Calcutta,
cages in Bombay and high-caste Brahmins, Rudyard Kipling,
while Kapil Dev scores the fastest century of the season,
a dark-skinned Tamil girl in Kuala Lumpur, but
I forget, we must travel to the east again.
Bradford is a little India of the North, they say here,
  the Yorkshire Mecca,
eating curry with our fingers, credit at local shops,
  and amazes my Argentine friend
but then Buenos Aires is far more European unlike Peru or
  Paraguay
countries through which I've travelled rough seeking what
  seemed alien.
I cannot remember much about Sri Lanka, December 1954,
except rusty gannets scavenging the harbour, bumboats
  selling pineapple and ivory,
redbrick public buildings that were probably British built
and a rickshaw round the temples, a fat Buddhist monk
showing us garish ikons of Gautama and begging a few rupees,
we ended up in a bamboo cafe with vegetable curry and beer,
the images are twenty-five years old, everywhere was strange
  to me,
I'm approaching that half-century and the world's not quite
  my 'oyster',
fears penetrate, there's less time before they close in and
  limit.

18

Sometimes I turn to those poems that first turned me on
    Sea Fever, Cargoes, Famagusta,
the novels of Dumas, Du Maurier and Margaret Irwin.
History enthralled for years, but then it was the Spanish
    Main, Renaissance Italy and 16th century Spain
and I recall one teacher who always spiced the facts with
    anecdote:
Lucrezia poisoned several husbands and with Cezare rolled
    in incest
while her father, the Pope, sired a hundred bastards (Tyrone
    Power in *Prince of Foxes*)
Catherine the Great kept a bodyguard of chosen officers
who serviced her in bed and when her appetite was jaded
    spanked the royal arse.
Nothing in the long term is forgotten, the past throws up
    its disparate material
in that private search for La Dorada.

Swimming the mile this afternoon I called each length a
    year of life,
the first thirty-six went quite slowly, the second half
    much quicker,
'*I do not count,*' she said. I find I'm counting all the
    time and always have done,
it's an obsession since number and quantity never equal
    quality
though there's some virtue in stamina and perseverance.

The waterfront with its bars from Hemingway novels,
blue crabs, turtles in tanks and conch shells,
over the hill into the black quarter fragrant with tropical
    blossom,
dusty tracks and sleek American cars and across the lagoon
    in a flat-bottomed boat
to Paradise beach — white sand green palms blue sea
    so serene and warm
it was difficult to believe that sharks occasionally
    entered the bay,
rum-and-cokes at a table under palms, *'big pricks are what
    women really go for,'* Robert said
after describing the genital dimensions of the sperm whale.
The women laughed at him, denying it. At sea in the bows,
flying-fish, a cool breeze, the banalities of drunken talk,
night clubs and bars no longer seemed to matter.
Betwen the coasts of Haiti and Cuba challenged by the radio
    of an American destroyer,
and into the harbour at San Domingo, in ruins among palms
an old cannon that once dominated the bay,
four days unloading whiskey and cigarettes, taking aboard
    sugar and coffee,
exploring the city and plantations, red flowers among the
    hills,
men with machetes, the aroma of burning rosewood, to
    Trujillo's house
a punk mansion with innumerable bathrooms
overlooking the southern part of the island, *'for orgies,'*
    the guide said,
but a puritanical emphasis upon cleanliness. Once more we
    sailed south,
the image of a *mulata* whore I followed through the docks
    like a grenadier his banner,
brown plump flesh in yellow silk all the way to Curaçao
    and the Gulf of Maracaibo.

Green the wooded valley of Red Beck, gnarled roots across
 the path
trees with grey squirrels, grass dripping from recent rain,
 mist over Shipley,
panting up the hill where six horses cantered over to the
 fence,
thinking of various women he's sent away when they've become
 too 'dominating' or 'possessive'
trying to impose their patterns on his routine, running
 the household,
but that's normal when people live together in domestic
 proximity
and perhaps he's unable to sustain a long-term relationship
fit only to live alone, a hermit at his desk or with his
 books
devoting an hour or two a day to friendship
not that he's disliked those who've gone, but having felt
 the threat of their demands
the inroads another makes upon the one they're with
he's ended it before the wine's turned sour, conflict re-
 placing what once was harmony.

It's not that I don't like argument or discussion
just that I want to be sure we're talking about things
 objectively,
that politics and bullfighting, the women's movement or
 literary values
are not concealing the real things at issue,
but watching Borg beat Tanner in the final, Navratilova
 for dessert,
cutting vegetables for the curry, music and friends,
something more positive was re-established.
Over to Heaton woods, walking past the reddened stream
 and sawn logs
trees in leaf, birdsong and rock outcrop,
making love as if to salve or salvage affection
 between her thighs
and banish the ghosts of lost love or that opposing quest
for *La Dorada* up the Orinoco River of fantasy.

21

We walked from Saltaire to Shipley Glen, a stolen car
　　maroon and beat-up
had been rolled down the green ravine, broken glass
　　and a view of the valley,
zigzagging through the golf course, up a stone-walled
　　track between farms
to the B-road winding to *Dick Hudson's* and Eldwick Crag,
　　over Bingley moor
the Twelve Apostles and old stone circle,
Denton and Blubberhouses way beyond, green ferns and
　　rocky crags,
triangles of gorse and copse, White Wells and in the town
　　itself
greeted by some Vietnamese boat-people, the girl in
　　traditional blue 'pyjamas'.
Others that day were being shot in Indochina
rammed by Thai boats and left to drown in the South China
　　Sea
marooned on the beach at Kuantan or in cattle-sheds in
　　Hong Kong.
'*It's a fucked-up world!*' We went to the Castle Museum,
read about the Roman settlement and Ilkley's conversion
　　to a spa
with the advent of that Victorian obsession — hydropathy.

22

I awoke from a dream that took me back troubled by
    doubt and regret
to that time I was in thrall to a twenty-one year old
who probably didn't understand in any way the spell
    she cast,
that is I loved and she loved, but both unwisely.
Walking at dawn through the woods, the sun a flame
    lighting up Windhill and Wrose,
the mills of Shipley in pink mist —
it's not her I regret, not now, not that amatory blindness
but the opportunities not taken while in that enchanted
    forest,
the people whose friendship I didn't pursue, the cowardice
    displayed
for fear of driving away or offending her,
that's the way it was and like a soldier at Flodden
I followed the bagpipes to my ruin.

23

We approached the thin green pencil-line, the sea so
    blue
'*Spanish waters, Spanish waters ringing in my ears*'
docked in Cristobal guarded by American soldiers, black
    iguanas in the monsoon-drain,
crossed the railway track into Colón, rats waddling along
    the gutters,
rickety balconies overlooking the dusty streets
dozens of *mulata* whores in bars, mini-skirted with dyed
    hair bouffant-style
demanding drinks, drumming sweaty fingers on beer-slopped
    tables
to the rhythm of the Beatles '*love, love me do,*'
stirred by tales of Drake and Henry Morgan, Newbolt and
    Masefield poems,
not wanting to reach Peru and teach...

(You should have been a merchant seaman like Conrad,
you should have been many things, but there are always
        limitations,
situations that provoke their unique dialectic,
record what was, or better still what is, you're in Bradford,
        short of money,
three kids and a woman who seems to love you,
the past is past is part of you, but keep it in perspective
        and in its place,
remember you cannot take one line of poetry or a single
        memory with you).
You crossed that narrow isthmus alone by bus, saw the ruins
        of Panama La Vieja,
the Pacific coast, made it back to that complex of wharfs
        and the *Salamanca*
headed down the Canal at night, the jungle shadowy and close,
heat rising off the land. Next morning in the lake with its
        red and green islands,
waiting to move down the Culebra Cut where Gauguin once
        worked with pick and shovel,
out into the bay at evening — a chiaroscuro of mauve, violets,
        blues and lavender,
10,000 seabirds following the ship on its way south.

24

Up the cobbled hill, the novels and the legend, to the
        parsonage
round the rooms — their shoes and dresses, the minute hand-
        writing in faded-brown ink,
overlooking the grave stones, the church and sweep of moor,
a sudden summer storm, beer in the *Black Bull*, Will Rowe
        restless
missing his children in Peru, Maureen putting her energies
        into translation,
broad hips and a plump arse in tight orange trousers skewer
        the eyes,
we're all obscured by our own problems
and standing in the rain I'm struck by the chronicles

that in this village are made more sombre by imagination
    and early death,
bronchitis and the body wastes away, those strangely
    talented sisters
their sexuality repressed, more a failure to recognise it
    for what it meant,
but let it all go and enjoy this walk, the B-road and track
    leading to the moors
where the Brontës spent so many hours,
over their bridge, taking photos, the literary associations
    a small frisson
but more this wild terrain and our walk to the Withens,
back along the ridge, past deserted farmhouse, sheep and
    stone cottage,
along the reservoir and into the village, a black mole in
    a driveway,
the day well-spent though nothing in our lives had changed.

25

Walking through Leeds, sudden exhilaration, the chaotic
    bookshop with its oddities and bargains,
a sense of a big city as distinct from a town,
with its myriad shops, districts, distractions and graffiti
to Headingley, fifth day of the Third Test after watching
    Botham's century on TV.
Two days ago I hired a car and drove the children south
    for two weeks
always this illusory sense of freedom that I've never
    actually experienced
alone, but I'm not, and if I were I'd search for company
    if only for an hour or two,
wary of giving too much in case that inspired exaggerated
    feelings and subsequent responsibility,
but driving back I missed the kids, they're not the shackle,
only my excuse for one, through the Vale of Evesham, plums
    at the roadside,
miles of orchard into Worcester, the cathedral where King
    John's buried,
the narrow-spired church above the Severn.

At Malvern — that odd group of hills on the edge of plain,
I climbed up to Worcester Beacon, sweating and short of
    breath,
gazed briefly out over a dozen counties, the fat farmlands
    of middle England
prized by Roman, Saxon, Viking, Norman and our 'Empire
    builders'.
Half-way along the saddle-back struck off at a tangent
down the clough, scrambling down through fern, bracken,
    briar and shale
braking hard on the thighs, heart thumping, sweat-soaked,
    head hot
to the car and M6, skirting Manchester, over the Pennines,
    home.
Now we watch cricket, books and beer in the blue haversack,
leave high on sun and alcohol, *you're so indecisive*
    and suddenly paranoid
waves of self-pity, that loser again — no money, no car
and Derek Randall in his publicity-car passes us at the
    lights at Kirkstall Lane,
twenty years ago I might have played professionally and the
    regret
for what was never attempted or achieved.

On the bus back through villages round the edge of cities
to Bradford where a cryptic note in the door brings me to
    my senses
are we all half-crazy, has the world gone mad?
Swimming the mile alone, thinking of the wasted time and
    experience gained
though most of its lessons learnt (like a straight bat
    and the narrow focus) too late.

26

OPEC raises its prices, 23 dollars a barrel, police have
    raided a house in Darlington,
where my illegitimate grandfather was once fostered out,
began work at twelve when Queen Victoria was Empress of
    India,
Gladstone and Disraeli vied for power, the Army was scattered
    round the Empire,
Stephenson's *Rocket* in a glass-case on the station, this
    house we live in now
had already been built, maids cooked on the black grate in
    the basement
and washed clothes in the shallow stone-basin at eye-level
    with the pavement,
stored food and wine in the cellar, coal under the stairs,
    rose at six each day
beneath a square of skylight, read by candle or gaslight
    in the attic,
wore long skirts and bustles, were corsetted by stays, big-
    buttocked,
the surreptitious stripping off and quickening guilt
a sense of sin and sweet pleasure stolen. But I'm wrong,
the switch stood in the corner, the offending flesh was
    cut and bruised
and *La vice Anglais* catered for in Chelsea brothels and
    flowery novelettes,
Swinburne, the public schools and colonies.

Manta rays, flying fish, a basking shark and a bottle-
    nose dolphin
scratching its back against the rusting hull as the ship
    glided through the brackish water
to the emerald coast and the lagoon of Buenaventura — *'the*
    shittiest port in Colombia'
but you liked it. Have written of it before,
black-and-green butterflies on deck, rats on the quayside,
    sweltering night and thunder near,
the whole bay lit and split by pink and violet lightning,
    rain sluicing down,
but you explored the town with its shanty bars and big-
    arsed whores,
the teeny boppers in that brothel younger than your
    daughter now,
clustering around you and chatting about the Beatles
because with your narrow jeans, fringed hair and blue-
    suede shorty jacket
you vaguely resembled them. Up the hill to Andagoya's
    statue
running the gauntlet of beggars, the Indian woman with a
    stump of arm
ragged and rickety kids, pink and lemon limousines over
    rutted streets,
pineapple, mango, papaya and green bananas in the stalls,
washing draped over the roadside shrubs and below —
    stilted huts
detritus on the puce-coloured sand, tin cans, old tyres,
    the rotting carcase of a dog,
but at night palm trees in silhouette, a moon on the
    white water,
the sound of children's voices and the thin strumming of
    a guitar.

28

Red Beck meanders along the clough
through woods in russet, gold and rust
gnarled roots crisscross the path,
        a narrow footbridge over it
above looking out to the mills of Shipley
plans for the immediate future
        some walking in the dales
places I've never seen and wish to.

The lights on Wrose Hill sheer up
        at the end of the street
glittering and orange in the cold night
a half-moon on the brow of the scarp.

Talk about pirates and buccaneers. Off La Libertad,
    Ecuador, a detachment of soldiers
small and brown in khaki-green boarded the *Salamanca*
    and held it to ransom,
the purser paid them off with a crate of Scotch and 200
    cigarettes a-piece.
Came morning and we were steaming up the jigsaw of the
    Guayas estuary
inlets, swamps, isolated huts on stilts, rusty water,
    jungle
to the port of Guayaquil, a complex bay, Chimborazo looming
    above green hills
snowcapped white, a sort of purity beyond the city.
Along the *malecón* with its arcaded pavement and decaying
    hotels of an earlier opulence,
the statue of San Martin and Bolivar. Here they had their
    rift and fracture
before liberating a continent, then exiled
dying in the obscurity of festering ports or Regency squares.
Beyond the hill — a giant molehill of shanties and higgledy-
    piggledy streets
the clean view from the top, then back along the rutted road
    to the ship,
Indians selling toucans, anteaters, bows-and-arrows, beads.

A perfect pale green twilight and a crescent moon while
     driving to the *Vaults*,
the same afternoon in Donegal a schooner sailed out of
     harbour to pick up some lobster-pots,
and was detonated by remote control. Four people died,
bits of wood and debris were washed ashore on the evening
     tide
and some hours later an army truck was blown up,
the survivors machine-gunned from the republican side.
I'm no blind patriot, nor admirer of national heroes
and read in *The Observer* of Baden-Powell's atrocities at
     the siege of Mafeking,
it's true, the Scout movement was founded by a sentimental
     racist
but today as we walk through the woods above Red Beck,
the sun warm in the valley, the moors in haze,
I expressed anger at all extremists who prize ideologies
     above the individual
'your heart is in the right place, but not always your
     reason,'
that the situation is complex there's no doubt, there's
     never an easy solution,
least of all through random assassination,
in Iran Kurds are being executed for 'making war on God'
a woman for adultery and prostitutes for practising their
     trade.
Nothing is more dangerous than a theocracy, theories of
     race,
the language of fanaticism that brings darkness to light
but were some maniac to harm my kids or jeopardise their
     lives
I *could* kill, drink wine from the cup of his skull, fashion
     a drum from his hide
and wear his scalp upon my belt as the Incas did.

SECTION 3

AUTUMN 1979

31

A green grape split open on the tarmac
loops of the Aire below the park
with its bandstand and red geraniums
'it makes you feel good just driving through this
valley'
the yellow buildings of Saltaire
and the pale olive of the moors beyond
from the top deck of a 624 Bradford Metro bus
    itself green and cream
bowling along over a couple of bridges
    towards Bingley
a scarp of moor high to the right
    and rising.

32

Sunday walked up to Peter's allotment
through binoculars the Aire valley clear
    in September sun
the hazy cinnamon of Bingley moor.
Imagine stripped to the waist digging here
planting potatoes, onion, carrot, lettuce,
    even red poppies
gazing across to the foothills and beyond
the house only ten minutes from such open country
    the wooded vale of Red Beck.

33

After a swim we walked to Bolling Hall high above the
    city,
once owned by the Tempest family, now a museum
inside mahogany and cedar, the four-poster bed and Tudor
    window overlooking the deer park
where Newcastle, the Royalist, about to ransack the town
    and put its citizens to the sword
slept, his cannon strategically placed,
'and every countenance was overspread with sorrow
every house overwhelmed with grief
husbands lamenting over their families
women wringing their hands in despair
children shrieking, crying, clinging to their parents
death in all its dreadful forms and frightful aspects
stalking every street and corner...,'
but he spared the town because of a midnight apparition
a female ghost (or whore sent by the citizens)
came to his bed, whispered *"pity, poor Bradford,"*
he heeded her plea, merely looting the place.
A generation later following the Restoration and the Plague
decline in the woollen trade reduced it to its customary
    poverty.
In the gathering light we walked downhill
looking for 19th century watercolour prints
by Crichton and others in odd corners of the city.

Lister Park is gold, russet and auburn, the valley down
    to the Aire
and the mills alongside the canal in autumn mist and mild
    sun
as we feed the ducks and geese on the pond.
The strange quality of Hockney's sketches in Cartwright
    Museum
that evokes eroticism at the edge of swimming-pools
California and Isherwood, Cavafy and Greece
and the realism of Stuart Hirst's paintings of odd and
    lovely corners
of this northern city, half-recognised streets of cottages,
snickets between stone terraces. It's the pluralism of
    society
as sociologists keep telling us. Bedi and Pervaz call
    round,
we eat chicken curry with our fingers. Bedi's poetry is
    possibly all aphorism and philosophic,
I don't know, Urdu is as foreign as the Punjab or Kashmir.
Tish and I make love, the sudden warmth inductive, her
    taste on my mouth,
the tang of chili that whets the appetite, garlic and
    beer on the breath.
Next day I walk to school to teach unwilling teenagers,
think of my daughter sailing from Hull to Bruges, its
    tangerine streets
and still green canals. I don't want to nag her, make her
    sullen and rebellious
or guilty of her pleasures. The fear of doing that nags
    me
as I see the corners of her mouth turn down, the child
    become the woman.

35

One night in the *Turf* we meet Nick for a drink
and he announces that Kay, his girlfriend, has split.
We're silenced for a moment — 'they seemed so permanent
    and suited.'
She's having an affair with Sue, the pop singer,
and Nick's being civilised about it, or trying to be,
he doesn't feel jealous, he says, not in the same way
    he would have done
had she been unfaithful with a man.
I'm reminded of the destructive dialogue in Hemingway's
    The Sea Change,
but what can you say to someone in such circumstances?
Only the drama of the moment holds us.
Stan tells him that he's a free agent now, but it's
    small consolation,
meanwhile at the Cincinnati concert of *The Who* eleven
    people have died,
my brother's lying on a beach in Bali or perhaps he's in
    Bangkok,
the world's a beautiful soft shade of blue when seen from
    the moon,
like many of us Nick's his own worst enemy, I think,
as another decade is drawing to its close
and I know less than I thought I did twenty years ago,
may even have been sidestepped by the pace of change,
three years ago when my wife had gone and my so-called
    freedom had begun to sour
it was the poems of Bukowski that forced the self-pity
    out of me.
Poetry is the only lasting antidote.

36

In the launderette a pretty Indian woman
red sari   green blouse   and bare brown belly
leans over the dryer piling in the washing.
Home the news is bleak — starvation in Cambodia,
        fanaticism in Iran —
turn it off, TV, the world
we're safe inside these walls, books on the shelves,
        food in the fridge.
I think of my daughter on a ship in the North Sea
dawns and sunsets at sea so many moons ago. Middle age
        looms
look at your face in the mirror after a day's teaching
        or hungover with flu imminent,
friends come round to watch the play — violence
        in the slums of Glasgow
and our private thoughts range over the past.
In bed we hold each other in the dark, I penetrate
        from behind,
her arse padding against my belly.

37

The Swale, the Ure, Nidd, Wharfe, Aire, Calder and Don
flow into the Ouse and the Humber estuary. We must tour
        this country
from Hull to Whitby, the North Yorkshire moors, walk the
        Pennine Way,
win the pools, write reams, publish and record,
study geology — limestone and millstone,
buy a car or bicycles at least, rewrite those fictions,
        get drunk only at home,
remain friends yet independent, never be dominated again,
live by our own code, stay alive, see the turn of the
        century.

The smell of sweat and tension in the examination-room,
Lady Macbeth taunting her husband for his cowardice,
too full of the milk of human kindness which is weakness
for not the meek, but the arrogant and ruthless shall
    inherit the earth
then calmly proceed to destroy it. Waves of hatred and a
    desire for revenge
reach me between the lines of my former wife's solicitor's
    letter,
her split nature, wanting it both ways, fire and ice,
to eliminate me from her life has long been her objective
    but of course she cannot
it must be like cancer of the brain, I've been crippled
    by it
as perhaps we all are, reading the poems of Hardy or
    listening to the news
it's all the same, The Third World cannot forget, neither
    can the blacks
slavery and the whip, nor women their centuries of bondage.
So we argue. The green mug with the Toulouse-Lautrec print
    shatters on the carpet,
I pass the hoover. 'Fascist, fascist shit!'
Forgive me for being blue-eyed, white, English-speaking
    and a male
but what use such a plea when the exploited rise up.
The mob will rule, I fear the mob — *a la lanterne*!
Driven to a corner the rat will turn, go for the exposed
    throat,
so build your walls and ramparts high, cut a moat and lock
    yourself in the North Tower
with a sword and longbow, the Red Rose lays siege,
Cromwell arrives, let the bombardment begin.

SECTION 4

WINTER 1979—80

39

Once again we drove up to East Linton, the Tyne,
white spume and a continuous roar through the gorge,
with Martin dug up artichokes and potatoes from the
frozen ground,
we drank mulled hibiscus-flavoured wine to see the old
year out
and the 1980s in. My brother wanted me to fight for the
tribesmen
in Afghanistan, I made no resolutions, voiced no hopes
except the silent one that we'd all survive another
decade intact,
drove home at dawn — a line of clear amber above the
North Sea
the sky an icy blue, no traffic on the road,
I thought of our walk to the old mill and back for Earl
Grey tea,
logs on the stove, conversation with friends,
a warm glow suffusing the fragrant room.

40

Walked up Bolton Hill, through the quarry, the church
    at Heaton and Lister's mill
sombre in mist on the far side of the valley,
through Wrose, skirting Eccleshill and down Park Road
    into a second valley
— this city is all up and down, long escarpments like
    archipelagos
thrusting through the suburbs once wild as any of the
    dales.
A white world again, trees under a fall of snow,
the possibility of a year abroad — Thailand or Malaya,
creditors breathing down our necks.
Stripped naked in the front room to the beat of *The
    Doors*
which turned me on, cursing the government, collecting
    old poems together
but publishers wilt, stringent cuts reduce the range
and the world news is ominous — '*I don't understand
    things anymore*,' you say.

Walking to school, snow thick on the ground,
I think I'm becoming pessimistic or more cynical as the
    years pass,
pretentious and mannered poems in magazines,
though Bukowski and Reznikoff maintain some hope.

41

Sleet and cold winds, vomiting bile and black coffee,
the bitterness expelled, bad dreams springing from
      solicitors' letters
that affect the subconscious through osmosis,
the gypsy's curse ringing in my ears in a plaza in San Juan
      — infertility and impotence
though minutes before she'd blessed my loins, the earth,
      my money
which like blood is dirt is shit is fertile.

We made love in the red glow of an electric-fire
but that fragile tenderness destroyed at dawn
pre-menstrual tension surging through the bloodstream.
Those islands — Java and Bali, the soft syllabics of Malay,
worship of the erotic, yin and yang,
saffron-robed priests in front of ancient carvings,
desire is suffering, its elimination perfect enlightenment.
A white world — symbol of mourning. Give me those Balinese
      gods.
If I write more I'll attempt a formal elegance.

42

The gypsy's curse boomerangs in the paranoia of alcohol
after watching Norwich and Liverpool in a 5-3 crackerjack,
the cave-paintings and papers in flames, fire kicked across
    the room
a scorched earth policy, black flakes of ash rising
and contrition between her thighs, mouth clamped like a
    limpet to the coral
'there's something in my nature,' it is ebony or jet,
exorcise it if you can, a chemical reaction in the blood-
    stream
filtered through the liver — sucked up by tube in that
    biopsy
dark and viscous, but in the morning all seemed so
    theatrical
a play we'd watched, nothing to do with either of us
though that evening — mango and pineapple fresh in the
    mouth
it was clearly there in the fragile mood.
Blame no one but yourself.

43

Flames above the millstone factory and the trees
leaping fiercely up, a pall of black smoke
and later the charred skeleton smouldering
ash and embers blown on the wind, the framework of girders
    bent and twisted.
Fear of fire gnaws at the mind at odd moments
gas explosion, short circuits, burning fat
and the kitchen full of acrid fumes and smoke.
Aries the fire-sign, but I prefer earth and water
though am drawn to energy and light, the fire that burns.

That afternoon we walked through Lister Park
past cascade and pond in warm sunshine
up to the hill where the looms whir and hum, weaving velvet,
trees in new leaf, lilac and cherry blossom,
    green and maroon,
the magenta fire of hawthorn in various gardens.

SECTION 5

SPRING 1980

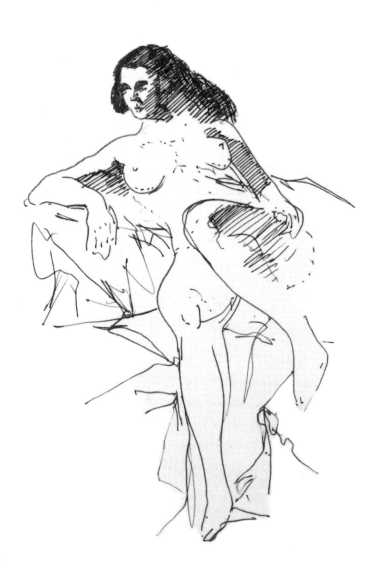

44

It was warm with blue skies — the Ides of March
and on the way home met the skirmishing of tribal warfare,
police cars, sirens wailing, zoomed along Manningham Lane.
We went to the match — City supporters penned in one half
    of the Kop,
Pompey supporters in the other chanting their slogans,
    winding each other up,
youths in braces, with crewcuts and boots, hurling abuse
    and threats,
close to panic police with dogs and on the green rectangle
    the football lousy
but at least we were in the sun.
Bedi cooked a chicken curry after several pints at the
    Royal
where the manager, John, ex-heavyweight boxer, read my
    article
and liked it though I often have such doubts...
Talking to Peter and wondering whether it matters anyway,
the vanity of it all, the hassles to be on the BBC,
to get this poem published and that book placed...
These March nights are dominated by TV, Australia and
    Thailand,
not envy but a desire to travel everywhere,
a miniature Buddha as a protective amulet against the evil
    eye or clap,
the saffron-robed priest preaching that all suffering stems
    from desire,
Ipswich beat Manchester United 6-0 and Mariner scores a
    hat-trick
'marvellous weather we're having, it uplifts you,'
eight more weeks of teaching, free then for the summer,
    out of debt and doubt.

45 'Things do do around Bradford'

after Gary Snyder

Reading and smoking in bed on lazy Sunday mornings,
making love to someone you know well, with humour and
    compassion,
walking up to Heaton and following the narrow valley of
    Red Beck,
cutting vegetables and preparing dinner, the radio on and
    the kids doing homework,
the glow after a mile swim at Shipley Baths, the view of the
    moors from the attic window,
the lights of Windhill on a frosty night or across the
    reservoir from Emm Lane,
the ochre churches and Lister's mill on the skyline seeming
    to rise from a sheet of water,
soaking in a hot bath after a tiring day, eating a huge plate
    of rice and stew
when you're starving, listening to the kids talk about
    school,
playing with the Siamese cat, stroking his white fur,
buying books for our personal library from second-hand places
    in the market,
watching rugby on TV and *Match of the Day*,
going to the pub for a few beers with friends on cold March
    evenings,
receiving letters from friends in distant places, getting
    a bumper post
magazines, acceptances, cheques, but no bills or bank state-
    ments,
old records on the stereo, typing poems at the desk by the
    window
overlooking the grey church, doctor's surgery, waste ground
    and snicket,
talking politics, our plans to travel while washing up or
    shopping,
writing endless novels in the mind while walking through the
    park,
going to the cinema on your complimentary tickets,
making a home and a life for the five of us.

46

Lying in the weak sun at Peter's allotment, the hills
  behind us
and the mill chimneys of Shipley, wanting to work the
  soil,
grow vegetables and become more self-sufficient,
drinking hot tea, a thin haze over the woods and Red
  Beck,
talking about poetry and football — arguments and anxieties
  recede,
dreams of travel, the misty green of that island
where Toussant L'Ouverture rose from less than nothing
— a black slave on a French plantation — to be the first
  architect of independence,
sold down the river by that power-obsessed emperor who rose
  from peasant stock in Corsica
"power corrupts, absolute power corrupts absolutely"
though walking through the pedestrian precinct in Leeds
to the bookstore selling poetry, you remark
that in *that* small world it helps at the moment to be
either black, Third World revolutionary or a woman...
Beneath the road tunnels menace with graffiti
'Hitler was right' and *'Niggers go home'*.
If there's an NF march in Manningham we'll counter-
  demonstrate,
if anyone were racist to Bedi — poet who studied Persian
  and Urdu at Lahore
we'd trade punches, make our stand against prejudice,
write our own graffiti for the oppressed
— this is not rhetoric, but common or community sense.

47

At the York meeting all those editors and pamphleteers
talking in endless circles about money and distribution
while West Ham were winning the FA Cup, I had to leave,
sat at a table by the Ouse and the bridge at Micklegate
and listened on the radio to the second half.
Last Sunday digging over the allotment in warm sun
stripped to the waist, the ground dusty on top with weeds
    and grass,
loamy underneath with pinkish worms wriggling from the
    sudden light,
a view of the valley and moors, an impressionist painting
    in green and blue.
All week the heatwave, England beating Argentina 3-1,
that silty river, rusty and brackish, blood-smelling on
    hot days,
the vast sprawl of the city along its banks
which these blue-and-white striped players in Wembley sun
remind me, Maradona knifing through four players,
then Coppell setting up a perfect Keegan goal.
All week heatwave and football in the evening on TV,
Wales and Leighton James putting it across England
    Saturday
as I wrote a section of my novel and we sat on the small
    lawn at the back
smoked cannabis, got high, the nectar of white wine
    on the tongue,
and made love despite our sunburn.

48

Last week I got a lift with Ian to London, hefting a
    heavy case
from Liverpool Street to Blackfriars,
met Martin who took me for a Turkish meal, then back to
    his flat in Luke Street
a block or two away from John Wesley's chapel and Bunhill
    Fields
where I paid my respect at the tombs of Blake and Defoe
    both seventy when they died
their headstones at right-angles to each other.
We talked till late *'I've never been myself with you,'*
I urge him to write more and put some money into the
    press.
We talk of numbers — the years, places, money and poems
    published,
marriages, affairs and women briefly known,
he knows the number as does Allan Burgis when I mention it
    next day
looking through his albums and correspondence.

After a soak in a hot bath I drink beer with my brother
    in Watford,
argue about politics and he tells me more about Bangkok.
In the morning, my birthday, I hitched up the M1 in five
    hours
and five lifts — one in a red Mercedes Coupe 3½ litre,
another with a mining-engineer who pointed out the pits
    en route
described disasters, said there were 300 years of known
    reserves
putting his faith in 'black gold' prophesied a boom.
After four days it was good to get back, I read the papers,
we went to bed, made love, then out for a birthday drink
    with friends.
Walking to school through the suburbs next day
I noticed a blackbird perched immobile on a wall,
it didn't fly away, I watched it for a moment, then walked
    on.

David Rock has illustrated books and magazines since 1950. He was born and educated in Sunderland and is a Partner in a national architectural practice.

He works and lives in London continuing not only illustrating but also painting and writing.

First published in 1984 by Rivelin Grapheme Press, 24 Aireville Road, Frizinghall, Bradford BD9 4HH.

Printed in England by Tony Ward and typeset by Bryan Williamson at the Arc & Throstle Press, The Old Fire Station, Rochdale Road, Todmorden, Lancs.

British Library Cataloguing in Publication Data

Tipton, David
    Wars of the roses.
    I. Title
    821'.914   PR6070.16

    ISBN 0-947612-07-6

This edition consists of 600 copies of which twenty-six copies have been lettered A-Z and signed by the author.

Rivelin Grapheme Press
London & Bradford 1984